FRED's
PERFORMER
ECTIONS

Hymns for Today

12 Contemporary Arrangements of Traditional Hymns

Arranged by Carol Tornquist

Again and again, it is written in the book of Psalms to "Sing to the Lord a new song." In arranging this collection, I had the opportunity to make some old songs new by shaping those timeless melodies into more contemporary settings. Each of these classic hymns takes on a fresh perspective by featuring syncopated rhythms, altered chords, and other unique effects. I hope that the new sounds in this edition only serve to enhance these songs that you have known since childhood.

May *Hymns for Today* be a perfect resource as you continue your ministry through music.

Cover: Waterfall photo © Morgan Firestine

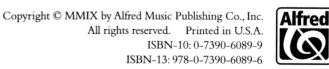

BE THOU MY VISION

Traditional Irish Melody
Arr. Carol Tornquist

Flowing, in an easy three ($\quad$ = 96)

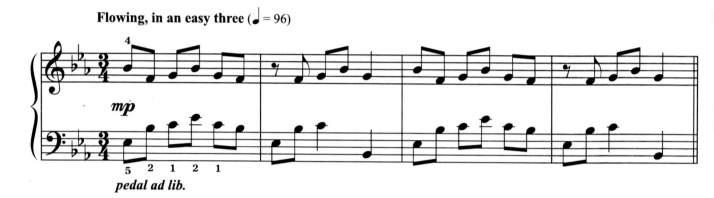

(Approx. Performance Time – 1:45)

COME, THOU FOUNT OF EVERY BLESSING

Traditional American Melody
Arr. Carol Tornquist

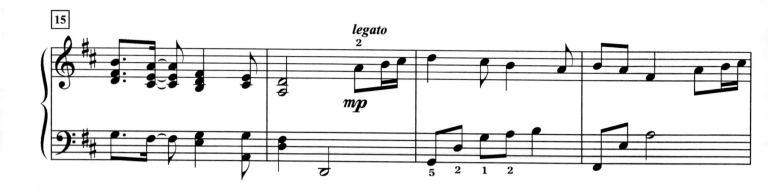

CROWN HIM WITH MANY CROWNS

George J. Elvey
Arr. Carol Tornquist

(Approx. Performance Time – 1:45)

FAIREST LORD JESUS

Silesian Folk Melody
Arr. Carol Tornquist

FOR THE BEAUTY OF THE EARTH

Conrad Kocher
Arr. Carol Tornquist

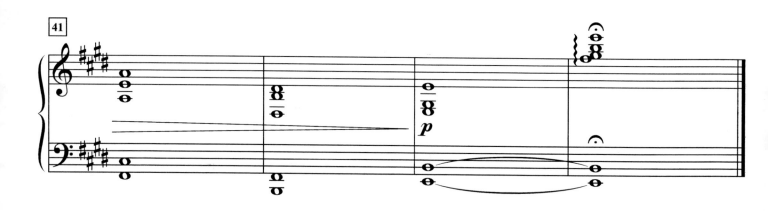

(Approx. Performance Time – 2:00)

HOW FIRM A FOUNDATION

Traditional American Melody
Arr. Carol Tornquist

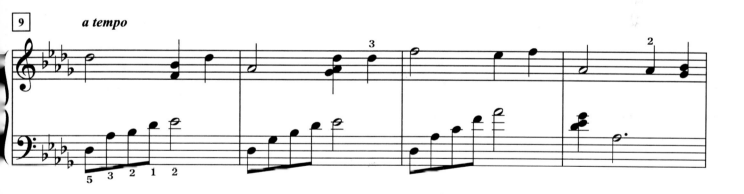

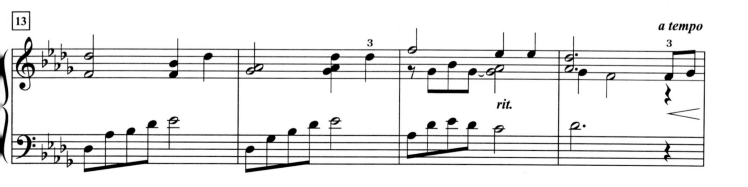

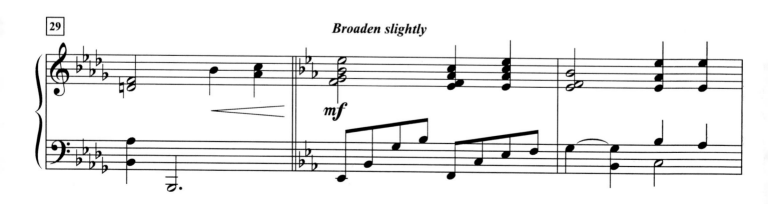

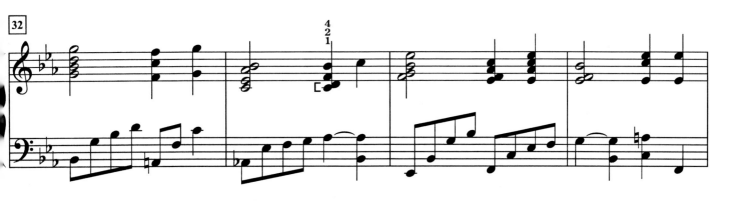

(Approx. Performance Time – 2:00)

A MIGHTY FORTRESS IS OUR GOD

Martin Luther
Arr. Carol Tornquist

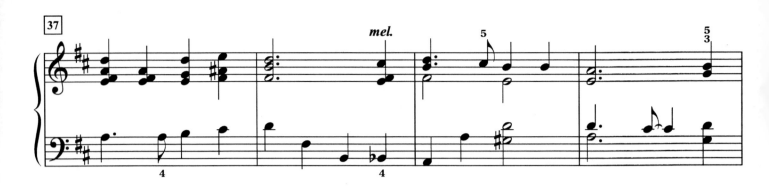

(Approx. Performance Time – 2:45)

MY JESUS, I LOVE THEE

Adoniram J. Gordon
Arr. Carol Tornquist

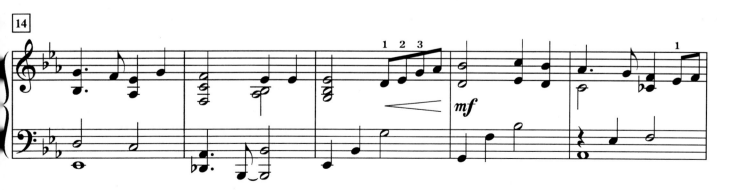

(Approx. Performance Time – 2:45)

NOTHING BUT THE BLOOD OF JESUS

Robert Lowry
Arr. Carol Tornquist

(Approx. Performance Time – 2:00)

WHEN MORNING GILDS THE SKIES

Joseph Barnby
Arr. Carol Tornquist

O the Deep, Deep Love of Jesus

Thomas J. Williams
Arr. Carol Tornquist

Flowing, in a moderate four (♩. = 72)

WONDERFUL WORDS OF LIFE

Philip P. Bliss
Arr. Carol Tornquist